KENTUCKY

The Bluegrass State

BY
JOHN HAMILTON

Abdo & Daughters

An imprint of Abdo Publishing | abdopublishing.com

abdopublishing.com

Published by ABDO Publishing, a division of ABDO, PO Box 398166, Minneapolis, Minnesota 55439. Copyright © 2017 by Abdo Consulting Group, Inc. International copyrights reserved in all countries. No part of this book may be reproduced in any form without written permission from the publisher. ABDO & Daughters™ is a trademark and logo of ABDO Publishing.

Printed in the United States of America, North Mankato, Minnesota.
012016
092016

THIS BOOK CONTAINS
RECYCLED MATERIALS

Editor: Sue Hamilton   **Contributing Editor:** Bridget O'Brien
Graphic Design: Sue Hamilton
Cover Art Direction: Candice Keimig   **Cover Photo Selection:** Neil Klinepier
Cover Photo: iStock
Interior Images: Alamy, AP, Bowling Green Hot Rods, Dreamstime, Florence Freedom, Ford Motor Company/Sam Varnhagen, Getty, Granger Collection, History in Full Color-Restoration/Colorization, iStock, John Hamilton, Jud McCranie, Kentucky Commission on Human Rights, Kentucky Native American Heritage Commission & Kentucky Heritage Council, Lexington Legends, Library of Congress, Louisville Bats, Mile High Maps, National Corvette Museum, National Park Service, New York Public Library, Science Source, Speed Art Museum, Steve Cook/Alex Lomas, University of Kentucky Wildcats, & Wikimedia.

Statistics: *State and City Populations*, U.S. Census Bureau, July 1, 2014 estimates; *Land and Water Area*, U.S. Census Bureau, 2010 Census, MAF/TIGER database; *State Temperature Extremes*, NOAA National Climatic Data Center; *Climatology and Average Annual Precipitation*, NOAA National Climatic Data Center, 1980-2015 statewide averages; *State Highest and Lowest Points*, NOAA National Geodetic Survey.

Websites: To learn more about the United States, visit booklinks.abdopublishing.com. These links are routinely monitored and updated to provide the most current information available.

Cataloging-in-Publication Data

Names: Hamilton, John, 1959- author.
Title: Kentucky / by John Hamilton.
Description: Minneapolis, MN : Abdo Publishing, [2017] | Series: The United
    States of America | Includes index.
Identifiers: LCCN 2015957606 | ISBN 9781680783193 (lib. bdg.) |
    ISBN 9781680774238 (ebook)
Subjects: LCSH: Kentucky--Juvenile literature.
Classification: DDC 976.9--dc23
LC record available at http://lccn.loc.gov/2015957606

CONTENTS

The Bluegrass State 4

Quick Facts 6

Geography 8

Climate and Weather 12

Plants and Animals 14

History 18

Did You Know? 24

People 26

Cities 30

Transportation 34

Natural Resources 36

Industry 38

Sports 40

Entertainment 42

Timeline 44

Glossary 46

Index 48

THE BLUEGRASS STATE

Kentucky is a land of contrasts. It is an in-between place that is both North and South, country and city. Say the word "Kentucky," and certain images leap to mind. Thoroughbred horses galloping through bluegrass-carpeted meadows. Banjos twanging on the front porch of an Appalachian Mountain log cabin. Barbecued chicken. Coal miners. Stately farms with white picket fences.

Kentucky has one foot firmly planted in the laid-back old South, with its other foot in the modern world. The state's bustling cities produce automobiles, fuel for power plants, chemicals, and textiles.

Kentucky's nickname is "The Bluegrass State." Bluegrass is a kind of meadow grass. It is not blue, but green. Its flowers are blue if allowed to grow to its natural height.

Bluegrass is also the name of a kind of music that comes from Kentucky. It is country jazz music played with banjos and fiddles. It's a friendly, toe-tapping sound that puts a smile on your face, just like the state of Kentucky.

Banjo and fiddle players perform during the ROMP (River Of Music Party) Festival held yearly in June in Owensboro, Kentucky.

QUICK FACTS

Name: The meaning of the word Kentucky is unclear, but it might be an Iroquois Native American word that means "on the meadow," or "prairie."

State Capital: Frankfort, population 27,557

Date of Statehood: June 1, 1792 (15th state)

Population: 4,413,457 (26th-most populous state)

Area (Total Land and Water): 40,408 square miles (104,656 sq km), 37th-largest state

Largest City: Louisville, population 612,780

Nickname: The Bluegrass State

Motto: United We Stand, Divided We Fall

State Bird: Cardinal

State Flower: Goldenrod

State Rock: Kentucky Agate

State Tree: Tulip Poplar

State Song: "My Old Kentucky Home"

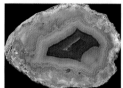

Highest Point: Black Mountain, 4,145 feet (1,263 m)

Lowest Point: 257 feet (78 m) on the Mississippi River in Fulton County

Tulip Poplar

Average July High Temperature: 87°F (31°C)

Record High Temperature: 114°F (46°C), in Greensburg on July 28, 1930

Average January Low Temperature: 25°F (-4°C)

Record Low Temperature: -37°F (-38°C), in Shelbyville on January 19, 1994

Black Mountain

Average Annual Precipitation: 48 inches (122 cm)

Number of U.S. Senators: 2

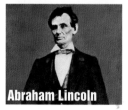

Abraham Lincoln

Number of U.S. Representatives: 6

U.S. Presidents Born In Kentucky: Abraham Lincoln

U.S. Postal Service Abbreviation: KY

GEOGRAPHY

Kentucky is in the east-central part of the United States. Many people consider it part of the South. It is the 37th-largest state, covering 40,408 square miles (104,656 sq km). At its widest points, Kentucky is 425 miles (684 km) from east to west. From north to south, it is at most 182 miles (293 km) long.

Kentucky shares borders with seven states. Ohio, Indiana, and Illinois are to the north. The Ohio River forms most of the state's northern border. The state of Missouri is to the west. It is separated from Kentucky by the Mississippi River. Kentucky's eastern neighbors are West Virginia and Virginia. The Big Sandy and Tug Fork Rivers separate West Virginia from Kentucky. Sharing a nearly straight border to the south is Tennessee.

Kentucky is covered in rolling plains, mountains, and forested lands.

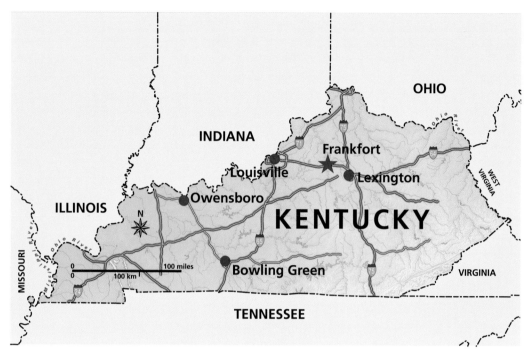

Kentucky's total land and water area is 40,408 square miles (104,656 sq km). It is the 37th-largest state. The state capital is Frankfort.

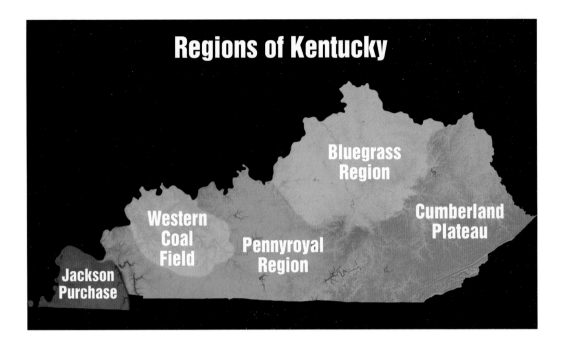

Regions of Kentucky

Kentucky has several different regions. The eastern third of the state is the Cumberland Plateau. The Appalachian Mountains are in this region. The highest point of Kentucky is here. It is Black Mountain (sometimes called Big Black Mountain). It rises 4,145 feet (1,263 m) above sea level. Besides rugged mountains, the Cumberland Plateau also has thick forests and rugged V-shaped valleys. One part of the Cumberland Plateau is known as the Eastern Coal Field because of its abundant coal deposits. Cumberland Gap is also here. It is a famous pass used by early settlers to travel through the Appalachian Mountains.

The Bluegrass Region is in north-central Kentucky. It is named for the grass that grows on the gently rolling hills and valleys in this part of the state. Most of Kentucky's biggest cities are in this region. Many crops are grown in the fertile soil. There are also hundreds of horse farms where Thoroughbreds are raised. One part of this region is called The Knobs. It has many tall, cone-shaped hills.

A view of Cumberland Gap, with Fern Lake in the middle. This famous, natural pass was used by settlers to travel through the Appalachian Mountains. Today, three states meet in this area: Kentucky, Tennessee, and Virginia.

West of the Bluegrass Region is the Pennyroyal Region. Also called the Mississippi Plateau, it has hills of limestone. There are many caves. In the region's northwest is the Western Coal Field.

The far west part of Kentucky includes the Jackson Purchase. It is a flat, low plain. Swamps, ponds, and small lakes can be found here.

Kentucky's major rivers include the Mississippi, Ohio, Big Sandy, Tug Fork, Green, Cumberland, Licking, Tennessee, and Kentucky Rivers.

CLIMATE AND WEATHER

Kentucky's climate is usually mild all year. The state lies between two climate zones, the subtropical and continental. Subtropical climates have hot, humid summers and mild winters. Continental climates also have hot, sticky summers, but can be very cold in winter. Kentucky is somewhere in the middle. It has warm, humid summers and cold winters with occasional snow. Temperatures are cooler in the northern part of the state. There is more precipitation in the south. Statewide, Kentucky averages 48 inches (122 cm) of precipitation each year.

Kentucky has four distinct seasons. Summers are hot and humid. The average July high temperature is 87°F (31°C). Thunderstorms are frequent. They sometimes bring high winds and flooding. Tornadoes are also a danger.

A September thunderstorm approaches a grain elevator near Henderson, Kentucky. With Kentucky's hot, humid weather, thunderstorms are common.

A woman walks her dog during a snowstorm in Lexington, Kentucky.

Kentucky winters are moderately cold. The average January low temperature is 25°F (-4°C). Northern Kentucky usually receives at least 10 inches (25 cm) of snow each year. Heavy snowfalls and below zero temperatures are rare.

Autumns in Kentucky are cool and crisp. Fall colors of yellow, red, and orange paint the hillsides, especially in the forested Appalachian Mountains of eastern Kentucky.

PLANTS AND ANIMALS

Kentucky's soil and mild climate results in a wide variety of plants and animals thriving in the state. About 48 percent of Kentucky is covered by forest. The most common forest type is oak-hickory. Red maple is the most common individual tree species. About 12 percent of trees in Kentucky are red maples. The official state tree, however, is the tulip tree. Also called the yellow poplar, it is one of the tallest trees native to the United States. Other trees found in Kentucky forests include eastern juniper, beech, magnolia, eastern hemlock, and eastern white pine. Cypress trees are often seen along the banks of Kentucky's many rivers.

Tulip Trees

Many kinds of flowers grow in Kentucky's soil. The official state flower is the goldenrod. It has a head of bright yellow flowers that grow in thick clusters. About three feet (.9 m) tall, it grows well in prairies and meadows. Other wildflowers native to Kentucky include purple coneflower, trillium, phlox, lily, and black-eyed Susan. Bluegrass is the official state grass of Kentucky.

A black bear peeks out between some foliage near Ashland, Kentucky.

The official state animal of Kentucky is the gray squirrel. White-tailed deer are common throughout the state. Black bears are often spotted roaming the hardwood forests of eastern Kentucky. Other animals commonly found in Kentucky include beavers, gray foxes, red foxes, raccoons, weasels, bobcats, chipmunks, opossums, river otters, muskrats, coyotes, and striped skunks. Millions of bats make their home in Kentucky's many caves. Elk, once hunted to extinction in Kentucky, have recently been reintroduced in the eastern part of the state.

Common reptiles found in Kentucky include fence lizards, six-lined racerunners, and several species of skinks. There are many kinds of turtles, including painted turtles, common snapping turtles, eastern box turtles, and softshell turtles. Common snakes include black racers, kingsnakes, corn snakes, rat snakes, and garter snakes. There are several venomous snakes in Kentucky to avoid, including copperheads, cottonmouths, and timber rattlesnakes.

Eagles and great blue herons nest by the Ohio River near Henderson, Kentucky.

The official state bird of Kentucky is the cardinal. The male has a bright-red coloring and a loud, whistling song. Wild turkeys are a favorite game animal for hunters. Other Kentucky birds include robins, doves, blue jays, blue herons, grouse, crows, Canada geese, and bald eagles.

Lurking beneath the surface of Kentucky's many rivers and lakes are largemouth and smallmouth bass, sunfish, northern pike, crappie, rainbow trout, brown trout, brook trout, and muskellunge. The official state fish is Kentucky spotted bass.

Great Blue Heron

HISTORY

From about 12,000 BC to 1650 AD, Kentucky was settled by the ancestors of today's Native Americans.

A Native American village in Kentucky around 1500 AD.

They used leaf-shaped stone spear points to hunt mammoths and bison. Some built communities. They constructed large dirt mounds for religious ceremonies such as burials.

After 1650, several Native American tribes struggled to control today's Kentucky. Tribes from the south, such as the Cherokees and Chickasaws, clashed with the Shawnees, who lived north of the Ohio River. Kentucky was in the middle. The Native Americans called the land the Great Meadow. None of the tribes could make it their permanent home.

The first Europeans to explore Kentucky were Spanish and French adventurers in the late 1600s. Traders came to the area in the 1700s. At this time, Kentucky was part of Virginia.

In 1750, a natural pass, called the Cumberland Gap, was discovered through the Appalachian Mountains by Virginian Thomas Walker. Thousands of settlers from the east passed through the Cumberland Gap, or rafted down the Ohio River, on their way into Kentucky.

In 1775, Daniel Boone blazed a trail into Kentucky. Settlers followed his path, which became known as the Wilderness Road.

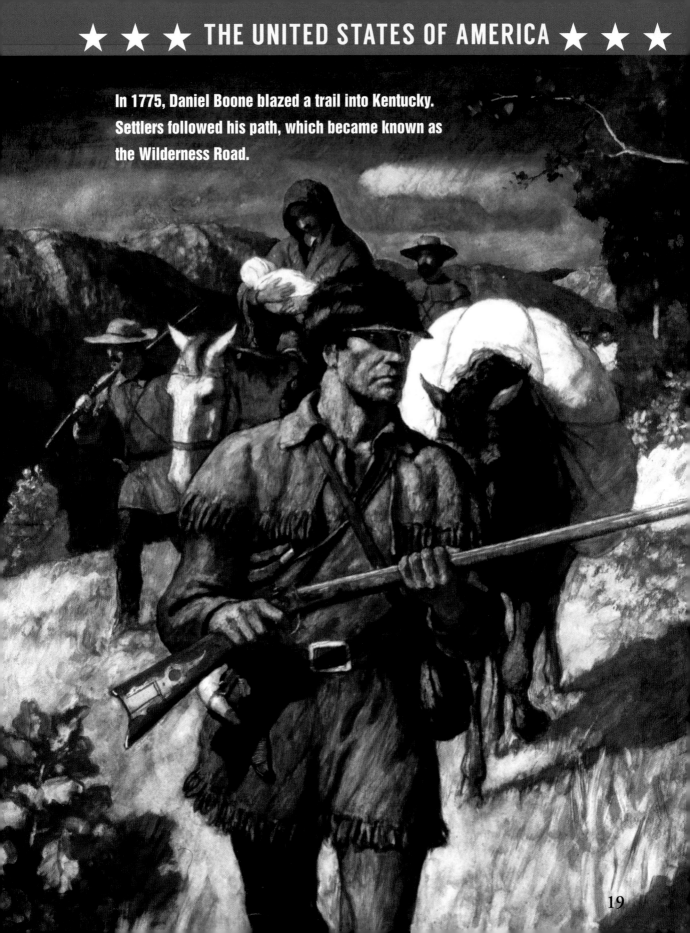

19

On August 19, 1782, a force of 50 British Loyalists and 300 Native Americans attacked American patriots near a Kentucky spring and salt lick called the Lower Blue Licks. The resulting clash became known as the bloody Battle of Blue Licks.

Fort Harrod was the first permanent European American settlement in Kentucky. It was built in 1774 by explorer James Harrod. Today's Harrodsburg, Kentucky, is named in his honor.

More settlers poured into Kentucky. Frontiersmen, such as Daniel Boone, blazed trails through the forests and mountains. Boone's route was called the Wilderness Road. Thousands of pioneers followed it.

During the American Revolution (1775-1784), several major battles were fought on Kentucky soil. Native American tribes, such as the Cherokee and Shawnee, also fought to keep white settlers off their traditional hunting grounds. The Battle of Blue Licks in 1782 was especially bloody.

After the war, Kentucky pioneers no longer wanted to be part of Virginia. On June 1, 1792, Kentucky became the 15th state to join the Union. It was the first land west of the Appalachian Mountains to become a state.

Kentucky's official name is the Commonwealth of Kentucky. "Commonwealth" in this case has the same meaning as "state." It simply means that it is governed by the permission of the people.

Kentucky's population quickly grew. Its location along the Ohio and Mississippi Rivers made it an important location for people and goods moving downstream to the west and south. After steamboats were built in the early 1800s, it became easier to move upstream also.

The steamboat Island Queen *approaches the dock in Louisville, Kentucky, around 1890. With all of Kentucky's rivers, steamboats were an excellent way to transport people and goods across the state and country.*

In the mid-1800s, citizens of Kentucky were divided over the issue of slavery. While many opposed the enslavement of African Americans, big tobacco and hemp plantations depended on their labor to make greater profits.

Kentucky was torn apart by the Civil War (1861-1865). As a border state, it was officially neutral during the war. Many Kentuckians supported the Confederate South, while many others stayed loyal to the Union North.

Kentucky was important to the North and South because of its waterways. Armies from both sides invaded the state. About 100,000 Kentuckians fought for the North, while 40,000 fought for the South. Several battles raged in Kentucky. The most violent was the bloody Battle of Perryville in 1862. About 1,600 soldiers from both sides were killed, and another 5,400 were wounded.

The North won the Civil War in 1865, but Kentuckians remained divided for many years.

The Battle of Perryville is also known as the Battle for Kentucky. After a fierce and deadly fight on October 8, 1862, the Union North won the battle. It kept control of Kentucky for the rest of the Civil War.

The High Bridge over the Kentucky River first opened in 1876, but was rebuilt in 1911. Designed to carry freight and passenger trains, it still stands today. It reaches 275 feet (84 m) over the river and is a National Engineering Landmark.

Railroads reached the eastern mountains in the early 1900s. Coal from the region was mined and shipped by rail. This paved the way for Kentucky's industrialization.

Kentucky went through many changes as its economy slowly shifted from farming to industry. Major businesses opened as new highways crisscrossed the state. By 1970, more people in Kentucky lived in cities than in rural areas. Today, new opportunities such as car manufacturing, banking, and tourism help Kentucky thrive.

DID YOU KNOW?

- Cumberland Falls is nicknamed "The Niagara of the South." It is located on the Cumberland River in the southeastern part of the state. Protected by Cumberland Falls State Resort Park, the waterfall plummets 68 feet (21 m). It creates a 125-foot (38-m) -wide curtain of water. During a full moon, when weather conditions are right, the waterfall produces a rare moonbow.

- The United States Mint stores much of the country's gold at a granite and steel vault at the Fort Knox Army post in northern Kentucky, near Louisville. The United States Bullion Depository was established in 1936. Today, it holds about 147 million ounces (4.2 billion g) of the precious metal. The vault is heavily guarded by a special police force.

- Kentucky has more river miles that are navigable by boat than any other state except Alaska. It is also the only state with three sides of its borders that are formed by rivers. They include the Big Sandy and Tug Fork Rivers on the east side, the Mississippi River on the west side, and the Ohio River to the north.

- Both Abraham Lincoln and Jefferson Davis were born in Kentucky, about one year and less than 100 miles (161 km) apart. During the Civil War, Lincoln was president of the United States. Davis led the Confederate States of America. Lincoln was born in 1809 in a one-room log cabin near Hodgenville, Kentucky. Today, the site is preserved as Abraham Lincoln Birthplace National Historical Park. Davis was born in 1808. His birthplace is marked by a 351-foot (107-m) stone obelisk at Jefferson Davis Monument State Historic Site in Fairview, Kentucky.

- Mammoth Cave National Park contains the world's longest known cave system. Its limestone tunnels stretch underground for more than 400 miles (644 km). There are many more tunnels that are unexplored. Mammoth Cave is in the hill country of central Kentucky. It began forming more than 10 million years ago. Rainwater seeped under a natural dome of shale and sandstone and slowly hollowed out tunnels in the limestone underneath. Native Americans used torches to explore the caverns about 4,000 years ago. European Americans first entered Mammoth Cave in the late 1700s. One legend says that a Kentucky hunter chasing a wounded bear discovered the cave entrance. Over the years, thousands of people have toured the underground wonderland. It was set aside as a national park in 1941.

PEOPLE

Muhammad Ali (1942-2016) was one of the greatest boxers of all time. As an amateur, he won two national Golden Gloves titles and held a record of 100 wins and just 5 losses. He won a gold medal at the 1960 Summer Olympic Games in Rome, Italy. During his professional boxing career in the 1960s and 1970s, he was a three-time world heavyweight champion. His nickname was "The Greatest." *Sports Illustrated* named him "Sportsman of the Century" in 1999. Many fans loved his brash style. He described his fighting system as "float like a butterfly and sting like a bee." Ali was born Cassius Clay Jr. in Louisville, Kentucky. He changed his name after converting to Islam.

Daniel Boone (1734-1820) was a hunter and frontiersman who explored Kentucky. His adventures made him an American folk legend. Born in Pennsylvania, he learned wilderness survival skills at a young age. He first visited Kentucky on a hunting trip in 1767. In 1775, Boone led an expedition into central Kentucky. He blazed a trail through the Cumberland Gap, a natural pass in the Appalachian Mountains. Called the Wilderness Road, Boone cleared the path and left markers, which made it easier for thousands of settlers to follow. He lived in a log cabin with his family at the end of the trail. The settlement he founded was called Boonesborough.

George Clooney (1961-) is one of the most popular actors in the world. He is also a film producer, director, and screenwriter. He has won two Academy Awards. One was for his role in the 2005 thriller *Syriana*. He also won a Best Picture Academy Award for the 2012 film *Argo*, which he produced. Clooney has starred in many successful and critically acclaimed films, including *Gravity*, *Ocean's Eleven*, *O Brother, Where Art Thou?*, and *The Monuments Men*. As a television actor, he is most famous for his role as a doctor in the hit series *ER*. Clooney is also very active in humanitarian work. He supports organizations that help victims of war and natural disasters, and was a United Nations Messenger of Peace. Clooney was born in Lexington, Kentucky.

Harland Sanders (1890-1980) is better known today as Colonel Sanders. His face is on every bucket of Kentucky Fried Chicken sold in 18,000 restaurants worldwide. Sanders invented his "secret recipe" for frying chicken in the 1930s. The first KFC franchise restaurant opened in 1952. He sold the fast-food chain in 1964, but remained as a popular spokesman until he died at age 90. Sanders was born in Indiana, but he lived in Kentucky nearly all his adult life.

Moneta J. Sleet Jr. (1926-1996) was a photojournalist who documented the American civil rights struggles of the 1960s. He documented many historic events, including civil rights leader Dr. Martin Luther King Jr. accepting the Nobel Peace Prize in 1964. In 1969, Sleet became the first African American to win the Pulitzer Prize for Feature Photography. Sleet was born in Owensboro, Kentucky.

CITIES

Louisville is Kentucky's most populous city. Its population is 612,780. It is in north-central Kentucky, along the shores of the Ohio River. Because of this, Louisville's nickname is "The River City." It is also called "The Falls City" because of the river rapids flowing through one part of Louisville. The city was established in 1778 by Revolutionary War hero George Rogers Clark. It was named after Louis XVI, the king of France. Today, Louisville is an important shipping hub, with many water, rail, and air cargo links to other parts of the country. Louisville is also a center for health care and manufacturing. The city is famous for the annual running of the Kentucky Derby horse race, held each May at Churchill Downs.

Lexington is the second-largest city in Kentucky. Its population is 310,797. It is in the north-central Bluegrass Region of the state. It is nicknamed "The Horse Capital of the World" because of the many Thoroughbred horse farms in the area. Major industries include automobile manufacturing, printed products, construction equipment, transportation, computer technology, and services. Lexington's largest employer is the University of Kentucky, which was founded in 1865. Lexington has a thriving arts community, including an orchestra, an opera, theaters, ballet companies, and many art fairs. The Festival of the Bluegrass is the state's oldest bluegrass music festival. It is held each June. The city was established in 1775. Settlers named it in honor of Lexington, Massachusetts, where the first battle of the American Revolution was fought.

Bowling Green is the third-most populous city
in Kentucky. Its population is 62,479. The city is located where the
Pennyroyal and Western Coal Field regions meet in south-central
Kentucky. Bowling Green is a center for health care and education.
Western Kentucky University is the city's top employer. Its sports teams
are very popular in the region. Other Bowling Green businesses include
manufacturing, clothing, and retail. Sports car lovers flock to the city
because Corvettes are manufactured at the General Motors Bowling
Green Assembly Plant. At the nearby National Corvette Museum,
visitors can see more than 80 Corvettes, including mint classics.

Owensboro is in the Western Coal Field region of northwestern Kentucky. It lies along the southern shore of the Ohio River. With a population of 58,374, it is the state's fourth-largest city. Owensboro is famous as the "Barbecue Capital of the World." Each May, the city hosts the International Bar-B-Q Festival, where more than 85,000 visitors can sample the region's best barbecued food.

Frankfort is the capital of Kentucky. Its population is just 27,557. It is one of the smallest capitals of any state in the country. It is located in the northern Bluegrass Region of the state, nestled along the shores of the Kentucky River. In addition to government, Frankfort is a trading center for agriculture and Thoroughbred horses. City businesses manufacture car parts, furniture, electronics, clothing, and machinery. Frankfort is home to Kentucky State University.

TRANSPORTATION

Kentucky is a center for transportation because of its central location and access to rivers. The state has 1,100 miles (1,770 km) of navigable waterways, one of the biggest systems in the United States. Businesses use the Mississippi River to the west, the Ohio River to the north, and the Tug Fork and Big Sandy Rivers to the east. Ships use these waterways to move raw materials and finished products to customers in other states. Kentucky has seven operating ports. In addition, it shares ports with neighboring states, such as Ohio's Ports of Cincinnati & Northern Kentucky along the Ohio River.

Kentucky has about 3,200 miles (5,150 km) of railroad tracks. Much of Kentucky's raw materials (especially coal) and manufactured goods are transported by freight haulers to and from river ports. There is also limited passenger traffic supplied by Amtrak.

A coal barge on the Ohio River passes under the George Rogers Clark Memorial Bridge between Louisville, Kentucky, and Jeffersonville, Indiana.

The Louisville International Airport is a UPS Worldport hub with the ability to sort up to 416,000 packages per hour. The facility covers 5,200,000 square feet (483,096 square meters), or about 108 football fields.

Several interstate and state highways crisscross Kentucky, making it easy to travel by car, truck, or bus. Public roadways in Kentucky total 79,598 miles (128,101 km).

Louisville International Airport is Kentucky's busiest airport. Each year, it handles more than 3.4 million passengers and 5 billion pounds (2.3 billion kg) of cargo. It is one of the busiest cargo-handling airports in the United States. Other major Kentucky airports include Blue Grass Airport in Lexington and Cincinnati/Northern Kentucky International Airport in Hebron, Kentucky.

TRANSPORTATION

NATURAL RESOURCES

Kentucky is one of the top coal-producing states in the country, annually extracting more than 77 million tons (69.9 million metric tons) in recent years. About a third of that is burned in Kentucky power plants. The rest is shipped to other states. Most of Kentucky's coal is mined in the northwestern and eastern parts of the state.

Much of Kentucky's coal requires digging deep into the Earth to extract. Coal found near the surface is strip mined by removing the top layer of soil. In the past, whole mountaintops were removed to mine coal. Today, laws require that the land be restored.

In addition to coal, Kentucky has many other mineral resources. They include sand, gravel, crushed stone, limestone, and clay. There are also minor oil and natural gas deposits in Kentucky.

A 2014 Kentucky highway project unearthed a coal seam near Elkhorn City, Kentucky. The coal was dug up and loaded onto dump trucks.

Spendthrift Farm is a Thoroughbred breeding facility outside of Lexington, Kentucky. Many of their foals have gone on to become winning racehorses.

For most of Kentucky's history, agriculture dominated the state economy. That is no longer true. However, even though manufacturing and service industries are now bigger, agriculture is still important. The state's leading farm products are poultry and eggs. Kentucky is the top beef cattle producer east of the Mississippi River. Other important farm products include corn, soybeans, tobacco, hay, and wheat.

Many of the finest Thoroughbred horses are born and raised on Kentucky farms. The state is often called the "Horse Capital of the World." Sales of horses produce more than $400 million each year.

INDUSTRY

Most people in Kentucky work in the service industries. They assist businesses and consumers instead of producing products. Service industries that are important to Kentucky's economy include banking, finance, and insurance. Retailing and wholesale trade are also big. Other important businesses include information technology, food processing, transportation services, and construction.

Many Kentuckians are employed in manufacturing. The state is a leader in automobile and truck assembly. Ford Motor Company, General Motors, and Toyota Motor Manufacturing all have large assembly plants in Kentucky. The state's rivers, railroads, and highways make it easy to transport materials and finished vehicles. Toyota's assembly plant in Georgetown covers 7.5 million square feet (696,773 sq m), equal to 156 football fields. Since 1988, it has produced more than 10 million vehicles.

Kentucky is a leader in automobile and truck assembly.

The International Bar-B-Q Festival brings thousands of people to Owensboro, Kentucky, every year in May.

Other products manufactured in Kentucky include machinery, chemicals, automobile parts, textiles, electrical equipment, and beverages.

In recent years, tourism has become a much larger part of Kentucky's economy. People come to explore the state's parks and resorts, or to enjoy the many music festivals and sporting events Kentucky has to offer. Tourists spend more than $8 billion in the state annually, resulting in almost 180,000 Kentucky jobs.

SPORTS

The Louisville Slugger baseball bat was created by Bud Hillerich in 1884.

Each year on the first Saturday of May, horse-racing fans turn their attention to Kentucky. That is when the world-famous Kentucky Derby is run at Churchill Downs in Louisville. Known as "The Run for the Roses," the Kentucky Derby has been the state's biggest horse-racing event since its first run in 1875. The fastest three-year-old Thoroughbreds in the country race for a distance of 1.25 miles (2 km) in front of more than 170,000 cheering fans. The winning horse is draped with a garland of more than 400 red roses.

Kentucky has a long history of horse racing. Besides Churchill Downs, other major racetracks include Ellis Park in Henderson, Keeneland Race Course in Lexington, Kentucky Downs in Franklin, and Turfway Park in Florence. More than two million fans attend races each year at these tracks.

College and high school sports are big in Kentucky, especially basketball. The most popular teams are the University of Kentucky Wildcats, the University of Louisville Cardinals, and the Western Kentucky University Hilltoppers.

There are no professional major league sports teams in Kentucky. However, the state does have several Minor League Baseball teams. They include the Louisville Bats, the Lexington Legends, the Bowling Green Hot Rods, and the Florence Freedom. Louisville is the city where the famous Louisville Slugger wooden baseball bat was invented.

The Kentucky Derby is a horse race held each May in Louisville, Kentucky. It is run at Churchill Downs. Three-year-old Thoroughbreds gallop around the 1.25-mile (2-km) track. It has been called "The Greatest Two Minutes in Racing."

ENTERTAINMENT

Arts and entertainment centers are found in many Kentucky cities. The Speed Art Museum in Louisville features art masterpieces from all over the world. The Louisville Orchestra was founded in

Speed Art Museum doubled its size with new buildings and renovations in 2016.

1937. It performs concerts throughout the state. Louisville also boasts a ballet troupe, an opera company, a children's stage theater, and Kentucky Shakespeare, which holds summer festivals in Louisville's Central Park.

The Lexington Opera House is listed on the National Register of Historic Places. It has been hosting world-class operas, stage plays, and concerts since 1886.

Music is an important part of Kentucky's culture. The Kentucky Music Hall of Fame can be toured in Renfro Valley. Bluegrass is a style that was born in the state. It mixes folk, country, and jazz. It is played with banjos, fiddles, guitars, mandolins, and other stringed instruments. Kentucky native Bill Monroe was a pioneer in developing bluegrass. Today, bluegrass can be heard in music festivals throughout the state. Lexington's Festival of the Bluegrass is an annual gathering for bluegrass lovers.

Kentucky is rich in history. There are dozens of historical sites to tour, including Abraham Lincoln Birthplace National Historical Park, which preserves the farm site where the future president spent his early childhood.

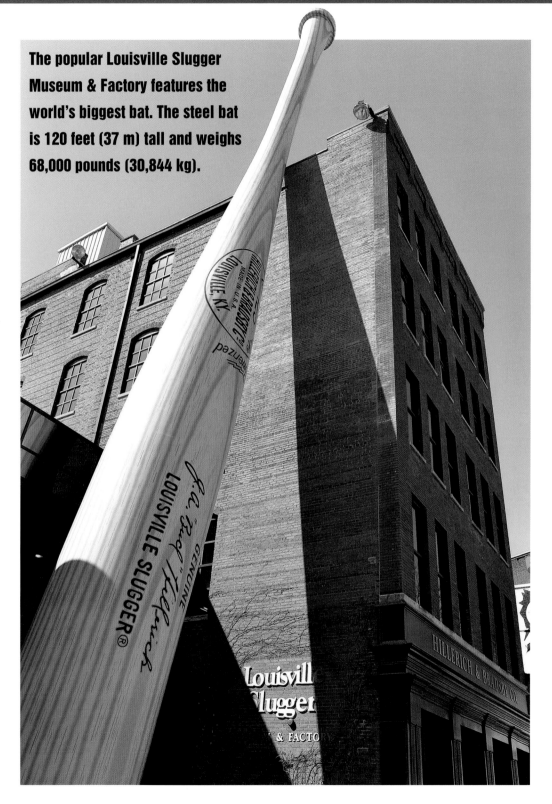

The popular Louisville Slugger Museum & Factory features the world's biggest bat. The steel bat is 120 feet (37 m) tall and weighs 68,000 pounds (30,844 kg).

ENTERTAINMENT

TIMELINE

1600s—Native American tribes fight one another for control of Kentucky.

Late 1600s—First Europeans explore Kentucky.

1774—Fort Harrod is the first permanent European American settlement in Kentucky.

1775—Daniel Boone blazes a trail through the Cumberland Gap and establishes Boonesborough.

Late 1770s—Settlers arrive in large numbers.

1782—The American Revolution's bloody Battle of Blue Licks is fought on Kentucky soil.

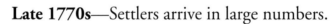

1792—Kentucky becomes the 15th state in the Union.

1810s—Steamboats begin traveling the Ohio River. Kentucky becomes a key link in the movement of people and goods throughout the country.

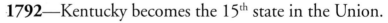

1861—The Civil War begins. Kentucky officially stays neutral.

1865—Civil War ends. Kentucky enters a long period of strife.

1900s—Coal mining becomes an important industry in Kentucky.

1950s—Manufacturing becomes key to Kentucky's economy.

2008—February tornadoes kill seven, injure hundreds, and destroy property.

2009—A January ice storm kills at least 24 people and leaves thousands without power for weeks. It is called the worst natural disaster in state history.

2012—University of Kentucky Wildcats men's basketball team wins the NCAA Division 1 Championship. It is the team's 8th NCAA Championship. Its 2011-2012 regular season record was 30-1.

2014—A sinkhole opens underneath the National Corvette Museum in Bowling Green, Kentucky. Eight classic and historic Corvettes fall into the huge hole. The unexpected disaster results in record-breaking crowds visiting the museum.

GLOSSARY

ACADEMY AWARD

An award presented to the year's best movie actors, writers, directors, producers, and technicians by the Academy of Motion Picture Arts and Sciences. It is also known as an Oscar, the gold statue awarded to the winners.

AMERICAN REVOLUTION

The war fought between the American colonies and Great Britain from 1775-1783. It is also known as the War of Independence or the Revolutionary War.

CIVIL WAR

The American war fought between the Northern and Southern states from 1861-1865. The Southern states were for slavery. They wanted to start their own country, known as the Confederacy. The Northern states fought against slavery and a division of the country.

CUMBERLAND GAP

A natural gap, or pass, through the Appalachian Mountains that made it easier for settlers to move west. The pass had been used for centuries by Native Americans. In 1750, Virginian Thomas Walker found the pass. He named it the Cumberland Gap to honor the English duke of Cumberland.

NOBEL PRIZE

An award given each year to someone who has made important achievements in a particular area of study. There are six awards: chemistry, physics, physiology/medicine, literature, economics, and peace.

PLATEAU

A large area of land that is mainly flat but much higher than the land that neighbors it.

PULITZER PRIZE

An award created by Joseph Pulitzer (1847-1911), a wealthy American publisher who owned several newspapers in the late 1800s and early 1900s. Today, Pulitzer Prizes are awarded in more than 20 categories, including newspaper reporting, feature writing, photojournalism, fiction, nonfiction, music, and drama.

RAPIDS

The part of a river where water flows very fast. The water speeds up because there is a sharp dip in the riverbed. Rapids can be very dangerous. Boats that try to pass through them can be greatly damaged or even destroyed.

RAW MATERIAL

Anything used in the making of something else. For example, corn is a raw material that can be made into a type of fuel for cars called ethanol.

STEAMBOAT

A ship that runs on the power of steam. The steam is used to turn a paddle wheel or a propeller that pushes the ship forward.

THOROUGHBRED

A breed of horse that is prized for speed and agility. They are most often used as race horses. Many Thoroughbreds are raised on Kentucky horse farms.

INDEX

A

Abraham Lincoln Birthplace National Historical Park 25, 42
Academy Award 28
Alaska 24
Ali, Muhammad 26
American Revolution 20, 30, 31
Amtrak 34
Appalachian Mountains 4, 10, 13, 18, 21, 27
Argo 28
Army, U.S. 24

B

Barbecue Capital of the World 33
Best Picture (Academy Award) 28
Big Black Mountain (*see* Black Mountain)
Big Sandy River 8, 11, 24, 34
Black Mountain 10
Blue Grass Airport 35
Blue Licks, Battle of 20
Bluegrass Region 10, 11, 31, 33
Bluegrass State, The 4
Boone, Daniel 20, 27
Boonesborough, KY 27
Bowling Green, KY 32
Bowling Green Assembly Plant 32
Bowling Green Hot Rods 40
Bullion Depository, United States 24

C

Central Park (Louisville) 42
Cherokee (tribe) 18, 20
Chickasaw tribe) 18
Churchill Downs 30, 40
Cincinnati/Northern Kentucky International Airport 35
Civil War 22, 25
Clark, George Rogers 30
Clay, Cassius Jr. 26
Clooney, George 28
Commonwealth of Kentucky 21
Confederate States of America 25
Corvettes 32
Cumberland Falls 24

Cumberland Falls State Resort Park 24
Cumberland Gap 10, 18, 27
Cumberland Plateau 10
Cumberland River 11, 24

D

Davis, Jefferson 25

E

Earth 36
Eastern Coal Field 10
Ellis Park 40
ER 28

F

Fairview, KY 25
Falls City, The 30
Feature Photography (Pulitzer Prize) 29
Festival of the Bluegrass 31, 42
Florence, KY 40
Florence Freedom 40
Ford Motor Company 38
Fort Harrod 20
Fort Knox 24
France 30
Frankfort, KY 33
Franklin, KY 40

G

General Motors 32, 38
Georgetown, KY 38
Golden Gloves 26
Gravity 28
Great Meadow 18
Greatest, The 26
Green River 11

H

Harrod, James 20
Harrodsburg, KY 20
Hebron, KY 35
Henderson, KY 40
Hodgenville, KY 25
Horse Capital of the World, The 31, 37

I

Illinois 8
Indiana 8, 29
International Bar-B-Q Festival 33
Italy 26

J

Jackson Purchase 11
Jefferson Davis Monument State Historic Site 25

K

Keeneland Race Course 40
Kentucky Derby 30, 40
Kentucky Downs 40
Kentucky Fried Chicken (KFC) 29
Kentucky Music Hall of Fame 42
Kentucky River 11, 33
Kentucky Shakespeare 42
Kentucky State University 33
Kentucky Wildcats 40
King, Martin Luther Jr. 29
Knobs, The 10

L

Lexington, KY 28, 31, 35, 40, 42
Lexington, MA 31
Lexington Legends 40
Lexington Opera House 42
Licking River 11
Lincoln, Abraham 25
Louis XVI 30
Louisville, KY 24, 26, 30, 40, 42
Louisville Bats 40
Louisville Cardinals 40
Louisville International Airport 35
Louisville Orchestra 42
Louisville Slugger 40

M

Mammoth Cave 25
Mammoth Cave National Park 25
Massachusetts 31
Messenger of Peace 28
Minor League Baseball 40
Mint, United States 24
Mississippi Plateau 11
Mississippi River 8, 11, 21, 24, 34, 37
Missouri 8
Monroe, Bill 42
Monuments Men, The 28

N

National Corvette Museum 32
National Register of Historic Places 42
Niagara of the South, The 24
Nobel Peace Prize 29
North 4, 22

O

O Brother, Where Art Thou? 28
Ocean's Eleven 28
Ohio 8, 34
Ohio River 8, 11, 18, 21, 24, 30, 33, 34
Olympic Games, Summer 26
Owensboro, KY 29, 33

P

Pennsylvania 27
Pennyroyal Region 11, 32
Perryville, Battle of 22
Ports of Cincinnati & Northern Kentucky 34
Pulitzer Prize 29

R

Renfro Valley, KY 42
Revolutionary War (*see* American Revolution)
River City, The 30
Rome, Italy 26
Run for the Roses, The 40

S

Sanders, Colonel (*see* Sanders, Harland)
Sanders, Harland 29
Shawnee (tribe) 18, 20
Sleet, Moneta J. Jr. 29
South 4, 8, 22
Speed Art Museum 42
Sports Illustrated 26
Sportsman of the Century 26
Syriana 28

T

Tennessee 8
Tennessee River 11
Thoroughbreds (horses) 4, 10, 31, 33, 37, 40
Toyota Motor Manufacturing 38
Tug Fork River 8, 11, 24, 34
Turfway Park 40

U

Union 21, 22
United Nations 28
United States 8, 14, 24, 25, 34, 35
University of Kentucky 31, 40
University of Louisville 40

V

Virginia 8, 18, 21

W

Walker, Thomas 18
West Virginia 8
Western Coal Field 11, 32, 33
Western Kentucky Hilltoppers 40
Western Kentucky University 32, 40
Wilderness Road 20, 27